UNBROKEN

A story of radical resilience, unapologetic healing,
and the fierce return to self.

JADE SALGADO

American Made Publishing

JS

UNBROKEN

A story of radical resilience, unapologetic healing,
and the fierce return to self.

ISBN 978-1-968175-00-9

Published by American Made Publishing Inc.
Boca Raton, Florida, United States

Printed in the United States of America.

First Edition.

For my son Aidan

who gave me the greatest reason to fight,

and for everyone who's ever had to rebuild themselves

from the inside out.

CONTENTS

Foreword   9

1 THE PAIN I IGNORED   15

2 THE DIAGNOSIS THAT CHANGED EVERYTHING   21

3 ONE BREAST, ONE DRAIN, AND A 5-YEAR-OLD   27

4 MEMORIAL SLOAN KETTERING & MY FIGHT FOR LIFE   33

5 THE WOMAN IN THE MIRROR   39

6 MY SON SAVED ME   43

7 I WANTED TO DIE (BUT CHOSE TO LIVE)   51

8 THE DECISION: NO MORE SURGERIES   57

9 THE WORKOUT THAT HEALED ME   63

10 TEACHING OTHERS, TRAINING THE MIND   69

11 FINANCIAL FALLOUT & MOVING TO FLORIDA   75

12 THE FRIENDS WHO CARRIED ME   81

13 FEEDING MYSELF WITH PURPOSE   87

14 FINDING JOY IN A SCARRED BODY   93

15 THE MIRROR, REVISITED   99

16 THIS IS WHY I'M WRITING   103

A Final Note from Jade   109

Acknowledgments   113

My Body, My Proof   117

FOREWORD

I Didn't Think It Could Be Cancer

How often do we assume that when something feels off in our body, it must be something serious? And how often do we ignore it anyway?

For months, I pushed through the pain.I was young. Healthy. Active. I ate well. I took care of myself. I had no family history. I had no reason, no data, to suspect anything life-threatening. I assumed it was inflammation. Maybe scar tissue. Maybe stress.

But cancer?

Never crossed my mind.

The pain started as a whisper, a dull ache beneath my left breast. I changed my posture. Slept on the couch for better support. Bought new bras. Juiced more. Stretched more. Took more deep breaths.

I told myself I was fine.
That it would pass.
That it was nothing.

Eight months later, it was still there.

Stronger. Sharper. Louder.

I could barely sneeze without wincing. I couldn't sleep on my side. I couldn't go a day without reminding myself to ignore my body's plea for attention. It wasn't until my implant had to be removed, and fluid began pooling beneath my skin that I finally got checked.

I went to see Dr. Bryan G. Forley, someone I had trusted for years. I wasn't expecting anything serious. Just answers. Maybe a correction. A fix.

But the moment he examined me, his tone shifted. He didn't panic. But he didn't dismiss it either. He paid attention. He asked more questions. He ordered tests most wouldn't have thought to order.

His focus, his intuition, and his willingness to act quickly became the first true turning point in my journey. Without him, I might still be waiting.

And by then?

It was already cancer.

Rare. Aggressive. Advanced.

And I had been walking around with it for almost a year. If I had listened sooner, maybe things would've been different. Maybe I wouldn't have lost ribs. Maybe I wouldn't have been left with scars across half my body. Maybe my son wouldn't have had to see me like that.

Maybe.

But this book isn't about maybes.

This book is about truth.

And here is mine:
I survived.
I'm still healing.
And I'm still learning how to live in this new version of me.

If you're reading this, maybe you are too.

And if so?

Let's walk this next part together.

UNBROKEN

CHAPTER ONE

The Pain I Ignored

I've always believed in discipline. In doing the right thing. I ate well. I exercised. I prioritized sleep. I drank green juice like religion. I was the "healthy one" in every circle, the one friends came to for clean recipes, the one who rarely got sick, the one who looked like she had it all together.

And yet, beneath the confidence and wellness routines, something was quietly beginning to unravel.

The first time I noticed the pain, it was a faint discomfort in my upper chest, almost like a tight sports bra or maybe a pulled muscle. It was subtle. Easy to explain away. I shrugged it off. I stretched a little more during yoga. I slept on my back instead of my side. I blamed it on stress, on motherhood, on life.

But the pain didn't leave.
It whispered first, then grew louder.

Over the next few weeks, it spread like a quiet thief, settling into the left side of my chest, between the ribs, near my heart. It was persistent, a gnawing, twisting pressure that made sneezing feel like an explosion. Still, I ignored it. Because that's what we do, right? Especially women. Especially mothers. Especially perfectionists.

I told myself I was fine. I smiled through it. I slept separately from my husband and son for months, curled on a downstairs couch with pillows stacked around me like a fortress, desperate for a position that wouldn't set my nerves on fire.

My son would ask, "Why don't you come to bed anymore, Mommy?" I'd ruffle his hair, kiss his forehead, and tell him, "Mommy's just more comfortable here, sweetie." He believed me. I think I wanted to believe it, too.

But the truth was: I was in pain. Daily. Deeply. And I didn't know why. Still, I kept going. That's what strong women do, right? We power through. We show up. We swallow the discomfort. We tell ourselves that if we can just get through the next day, or the next week, it'll get better.

But it didn't.

And then, one morning, as I was brushing my hair in the bathroom mirror, I caught a glimpse of myself, not physically, but emotionally. I saw a woman pretending. Pretending the pain wasn't real. Pretending she had control. Pretending everything was okay.

That moment sat with me for days.

But I still waited.

Eight months.

Eight months of playing tug-of-war with my instincts. One voice whispering, "Get checked," and the other louder one shouting, "You're overreacting. You're fine. Don't be dramatic. You're probably just hormonal or tired or tense!"

What I didn't realize then is that I was gaslighting myself. I was the one invalidating my own pain.

In hindsight, I wonder: what if I had listened to that quiet voice sooner? What if I had put my pride aside and scheduled that doctor's appointment at the first sign of something wrong?

Would I still have all of my ribs?

Would I still have both breasts?

Would I still feel whole?

That's the thing about illness, it doesn't always announce itself with sirens. Sometimes, it arrives like fog; slowly, invisibly, until you realize you can no longer see the road ahead.

Eventually, the pain escalated to the point where I couldn't ignore it anymore. Every breath became a reminder that something was deeply wrong. I couldn't laugh without wincing. Couldn't sneeze without bracing myself against the wall.

I finally made the appointment with Dr. Bryan G. Forley, the plastic surgeon I'd trusted for years. Even then, I wasn't thinking "cancer." Maybe scar tissue. Maybe a bad implant. I thought we'd remove the implant, take a peek, and fix whatever had shifted inside me.

What we found was nothing. No visual sign of disease. So, a new implant was placed in, and I went home.

But my body wasn't done screaming.

Days later, my breast swelled unnaturally. My skin pulled tight. The stitches burst open. I was back in Dr. Forley's office, this time to remove the implant and insert a surgical drain to manage the fluid that wouldn't stop accumulating. He decided, cautiously, to send samples for biopsy.

At that point, I was still functioning, taking care of my son, cooking dinners, folding laundry, picking him up from school. But underneath the routine, something in me had cracked. I had been living in a body that was begging to be heard, and I had silenced it for nearly a year.

When the biopsy came back, everything changed.

But that's the next chapter.

This one ends with a woman sitting alone on a couch, night after night, clutching her ribs, praying the pain was nothing. Hoping her strength could override biology.

And learning, far too late, that **hope is not a medical plan**.

CHAPTER TWO

The Diagnosis That Changed Everything

The word cancer didn't crash into my life with panic or fear. It landed with silence. With focus. With purpose.

When Dr. Forley told me the biopsy results, I didn't cry. I didn't ask, "Why me?" I didn't crumble under the weight of the word. I simply listened. Absorbed. Calculated.

Squamous cell carcinoma. Aggressive. Rare. Advanced.

It was a lot to process, yes. But not because I was scared.

I was never afraid.

Instead, a deep calm settled over me. My mind went into work mode. What's next? What does this mean? Who do I need to talk to? How do we fight this? Even before I had all the facts, I was already building a battle plan.

I left Dr. Forley's office with the weight of a new reality, but no panic. That has never been my way. I don't do despair. I don't waste time on blame. When the fight comes, I show up.

But even in that storm of new information and emotion, I

remember feeling one thing with crystal clarity: gratitude for Dr. Forley. He could have dismissed my pain like so many others might have. He could have stopped at the obvious, the swelling, the discomfort, the implant complications. But he didn't.

He paid attention. He trusted his instincts. He acted quickly. He didn't just give me a diagnosis. He gave me time. And in a journey where time is everything, that gift was immeasurable.

Most doctors would've considered their role complete after surgery. But he didn't step away. He stayed involved. He stayed invested. He made sure I wasn't just a patient, I was seen.

The days that followed were full of scans, bloodwork, and terms I'd never used before. MRI. CT. PET. Staging. Protocol. Suddenly, I was the center of a whirlwind of logistics and appointments. My life, which had once been ruled by school pickups and green smoothies, was now measured in test results and clinical reports.

That's when I met Dr. Paul Tartter, a breast cancer specialist in New York City. It was freezing cold that day, one of those mornings that smells like snow before it even falls. I went alone. Not because I didn't have support, but because I needed my mind clear, unclouded. I didn't want to manage anyone else's emotions. I wanted to focus. To understand.

Dr. Tartter didn't waste time. He pulled up my PET scan and showed me what had been hiding inside me: the cancer had wrapped around my left chest wall, eaten away at my ribs, and was pressing dangerously close to my heart. My entire left side glowed on the scan like a warning light.

It was intense. Concerning. Complicated.

He looked at me with steady eyes and said, "I've never seen anything like this before." He told me honestly, he couldn't treat it. It was beyond his scope.

But he didn't leave me hanging. Right there, in front of me, he picked up the phone and called Memorial Sloan Kettering Cancer Center. Dr. Sharlotte Ariyan answered, and within minutes, my next step was secured.

There was no time to fall apart, not that I would've. That's not who I am. After the appointment, I climbed into a yellow cab and made my way to a hotel near the Throgs Neck Bridge. I couldn't go home yet. The radioactive materials from the PET scan meant I had to stay away from my son for 24 hours.

That hotel room was the first time I was truly alone with the news.

And even then, I didn't fall apart.

Yes, I cried. Yes, the pain from the drain was unbearable that night. Yes, I felt the weight of the journey ahead. But I didn't feel like a victim. I didn't feel broken. I wasn't waiting to be rescued.

I was gathering my strength.

That night, I let my tears fall. Not out of fear, but out of release. A physical response to the knowledge that the fight had officially begun. This wasn't grief. This wasn't panic. This was the body processing what the mind had already accepted:

You have cancer. Now let's handle it.

The next morning, I returned home. I hugged my son. I kissed my husband. I put on a smile, not a fake one, but one built from resolve. When I told my husband the full truth that night, we didn't fall apart together. We leaned in. We made a pact.

We would do this as a team. We would carry each other when the other got tired. But we would never let cancer be bigger than us.

This was no longer just a medical situation. This was war.

And I've always been a fighter.

I wasn't waiting for someone to save me.

I was already saving myself.

CHAPTER THREE

One Breast, One Drain, and a 5-Year-Old

You don't realize how much your body does until it stops doing it. Simple things; lifting your child, turning in bed, putting on a shirt, become victories. Showers become calculated. Sleep becomes performance art. And dignity? Well, that gets redefined completely.

I was now a woman with a drain stitched to my chest and one breast. Every movement reminded me that I was in a different chapter of my life. There was no easing into this reality. There was no ramp-up. One day I was sipping green juice, and the next I was draining fluid from my body into a plastic bulb clipped to my bra strap.

But I wasn't fragile.

I still made dinner. I still folded laundry. I still kissed my son goodnight. I still showed up, even when my body showed signs of giving out.

My son was five. Too young to understand what cancer was, but old enough to sense something was wrong. Kids have a radar for their parents' unspoken truths. They see past the words. They feel the shift in energy. And mine, my sweet boy, had already noticed.

"Mommy, how come you don't go to bed with Daddy anymore?"

His eyes were wide. Innocent. Curious. Not scared, just searching for truth.

I smiled gently, tucking a blanket around his little legs. "Mommy's chest is a little sore right now, so I'm sleeping downstairs until I feel better."

He nodded, accepting it the way kids do, because the person telling him was calm. Because I didn't flinch. Because in our house, Mommy's strength was never in question.

But I was in pain. Deep, biting pain that made it hard to breathe, hard to hug, hard to laugh. I slept on the couch because the incline helped me breathe. The drain in my chest had to be propped a certain way. And upstairs, where our bedroom was, might as well have been Everest.

Still, I kept routines going.

I made his lunch. Brushed his hair. Walked him to the door for school pickup. He never saw me crumble. I wouldn't allow it.

The hardest part wasn't the diagnosis. It wasn't the drain or the swelling or the deep ache in my bones.

The hardest part was pretending like nothing was wrong in

front of the one person I never wanted to worry.

My son.

When you're a mother fighting cancer, you don't just battle disease, you battle guilt. You wrestle with the days you're too tired to play, the nights you can't tuck them in, the hours spent at appointments instead of the playground.

But kids, they forgive faster than adults. They don't count the absences. They remember the way you look at them. The sound of your voice. The energy of your love.

And I gave him all of it.

Even when I had nothing left for myself.

When the results came back and it was confirmed that I had an aggressive form of cancer, life went from heavy to surgical. Plans had to be made. Tests needed to be booked. MSK became a second home.

But the drain stayed.

I wore it everywhere. To school drop-offs, to the grocery store, to the couch where I slept most nights. I learned how to clean it, dress it, drain it. I became my own nurse. And I did it all with one goal in mind: to stay present for my son.

He never knew the full extent of what was happening. We kept it age-appropriate. Simple.

When I started chemo, I still had my hair for a little while. But after that first long stint in the hospital, 13 days of isolation and testing, everything changed. I came home looking different.

Thinner. Paler. Tired.

And that day, I shaved my head.

He came home from school, dropped his backpack, and froze. He stared at me.

"Mommy, what happened to your beautiful long hair?"

I knelt in front of him and took his hands. "The medicine made me sick, baby. My hair started falling out, so I shaved it. But guess what? It's going to grow all the way back down to my butt."

He blinked, confused, then suddenly burst into laughter.

"You said butt!"

And just like that, the moment transformed.

We were laughing. Crying and laughing. I was holding him in my arms while a drain pressed between us, while my chest ached, while everything in the world was unrecognizable. But for that moment, it felt normal.

This was the rhythm of life now. Pain. Resilience. Laughter. Fatigue. Survival. My body was being dismantled piece by piece, but I was still mothering. Still anchoring my home with love and fire.

And when I look back on that season of my life, the months with one breast, the drain, the pain. I don't see suffering.

I see strength.

Not the kind that shouts. The kind that whispers through lullabies and bedtime stories and walks to the kitchen, drain and all, to make pancakes on a Saturday morning.

That was me.

One breast. One drain. One five-year-old who needed his mom.

And I never let cancer take that away.

CHAPTER FOUR

Memorial Sloan Kettering & My Fight for Life

There are names that become part of your story whether you choose them or not. For me, one of those names is Memorial Sloan Kettering. I had heard of it, of course. It was the cancer hospital in New York. People traveled from all over the world to be treated there. But it never once crossed my mind that I would be one of those people. Until suddenly, I was.

Dr. Tartter had made the call personally, a moment I'll never forget. There was a level of urgency in his voice I hadn't heard before. When he hung up, he looked at me with something between resolve and hesitation. "They'll take you," he said. "Dr. Sharlotte Ariyan wants to see you right away."

I nodded. "Okay. Let's go."

I wasn't afraid. I wasn't Overwhelmed. I was focused. I had cancer, yes. But I also had clarity. This was the next move on the board. And I was ready to make it.

The morning of my first visit to MSK, I woke up early. The city was gray and cold, a blanket of wind moving through the streets like it had somewhere to be. I dressed carefully, soft layers over a body that was already tender, protective of the drain still stitched into my chest.

My husband drove me. He always did. Every appointment, every test, every terrifying unknown, he was behind the wheel, beside me, in step with me. He held the wheel while I held my strength.

As we drove into the city, I stared out the window at New York like I was seeing it for the first time. People rushing. Horns blaring. Coffee cups steaming through gloved hands. It was the same city I'd always known, but I was seeing it now through the eyes of a woman whose body had declared war.

And I was bringing that war to the front lines.

Memorial Sloan Kettering.

A place where battles were fought, and won.

And I wouldn't have even gotten there if it weren't for Dr. Forley. He could've stepped away after the biopsy, after the second implant removal, after confirming what most surgeons would consider "outside their lane." But he didn't. He stayed involved. He stayed in the conversation. He didn't just refer me to MSK. He opened the door, held it, and walked beside me until I was through it.

He checked in after the fact. He followed my progress. He cared about what happened next.

That kind of follow-through isn't common in medicine. But it's exactly who he is. Quiet support. Steady presence. He wasn't just the beginning of my diagnosis, he was a thread that stayed woven into the entire journey.

Dr. Sharlotte Ariyan greeted me with compassion and calm precision. She didn't sugarcoat things. She didn't try to soften the blow. She respected my intelligence, my strength, and most of all, my agency. That mattered to me.

I wasn't looking for pity. I wasn't here for handholding.

I was here for answers.

She brought in a team of doctors, specialists from every angle. Each one stared at my case with the same expression: curiosity and concern.

My cancer was rare. Complex. Not easily defined by protocols or past cases. There was no clear path forward. Just possibilities. Risk. Strategy.

And yet, I wasn't scared.

I was hungry to learn.

Every word, every scan, every diagram they showed me, I wanted to understand it. I wanted to know what we were up against. I wasn't passive in this process. I was the commander of it. This was my body. This was my fight.

I asked questions. I took notes. I listened with a laser focus.

And when the plan became clear, to begin chemotherapy immediately in order to stop the spread and stabilize my condition, I didn't hesitate.

Let's begin.

Treatment at MSK wasn't just about the medicine. It was about the atmosphere — this world where hope and heartbreak sat side by side in the waiting room. Where you could look into the eyes of a stranger and see your own reflection, the pain, the determination, the silent prayers playing behind the eyes.

I came in every week, sometimes multiple times aweek, depending on the schedule. Some appointments were routine, others terrifying. There were moments when the weight of what was happening hit me physically, not emotionally, but in my bones. Like my body was metabolizing grief and resolve at the same time.

But no matter what the scans said, no matter how many needles, tests, or days of vomiting I endured, I kept my rhythm.

I was still a mother. Still a wife. Still me.

I would finish chemo, step outside, and call my son's school to check on a field trip. I would answer emails. Cook dinner. Clean up Legos.

Cancer didn't make me a different woman.

It revealed who I had always been.

There were moments, of course, that tested me. There were nights I lay in bed, staring at the ceiling, wondering how much more I could take.

But never once did I ask, Why me?

Because I never believed this was punishment. It wasn't karma. It wasn't fate. It was just life. And life doesn't owe you easy. It owes you nothing. But if you meet it with fire and fight, it will show you what you're made of.

And MSK became the place where I began to see just how much strength I carried in this body, even with parts of it missing.

One day, after a particularly difficult round of chemo, I remember stepping into the elevator and catching my reflection in the mirror. It stared back at me; pale, bald, thin, and scarred.

But also alive.
Standing. Moving. Fighting.

I smiled at myself.
Because this woman?
She wasn't broken.
She was a warrior in motion.

CHAPTER FIVE
The Woman in the Mirror

The body I once lived in is gone. Literally. I don't mean metaphorically. The curves, the symmetry, the softness, the familiar way I used to recognize myself in the mirror, all of it, altered.

My body became a battlefield. And like any battlefield, it bore the evidence: scars, stitches, skin grafts, pieces missing and others reshaped.

I used to stand in the mirror and trace the lines of my figure with pride. I saw a woman who was strong, radiant, feminine. The body I had built through clean eating, consistent training, and discipline had always been a source of confidence.

But now? Now, I avoided mirrors altogether.

Not because I couldn't face what was there. But because I didn't recognize it. It was like waking up one day in someone else's skin. Not out of shame. Not out of fear. But out of sheer unfamiliarity.

This body didn't move the same. Didn't breathe the same. Didn't rest the same. After the last major surgery, I remember standing in front of the mirror in my bedroom, just standing there, frozen. I had seen my reflection a thousand times. But this time, I looked deeper. Past the skin. Past the wounds. Past the missing pieces.

I asked myself a question I wasn't ready to answer:

"Can I love this body now?"

Not tolerate it.
Not endure it.
Love it.

That question lived in me for weeks.

I stopped asking whether I would go back for more procedures. That wasn't the point anymore. The point was: could I exist fully, emotionally, spiritually, and intimately, in the body I had right now?

My husband and I talked late into the night during those weeks. He told me I was beautiful. Not in spite of the scars, but because of the strength behind them. He told me I didn't have to do anything else to be whole.

"You already are," he said.

And even though part of me wanted to believe it… I had to come to that conclusion for myself.

So I started showing up differently. I stopped hiding in

baggy clothes. I started moving again, gently, intentionally. I placed my hand on the parts of my body I used to avoid and whispered, "Thank you" instead of "Why?"

I started smiling at my reflection again. Not because I liked everything I saw, but because I was still here. And that meant something.

There were still hard days.

Still moments where I flinched at my reflection or avoided catching myself in a window.

But those moments became fewer.

Because self-love isn't a one-time event. It's not a Pinterest quote or a yoga retreat. It's a practice. A discipline. A decision you make every single day to see yourself through eyes of compassion and courage.

And one day, quietly, powerfully, I looked in the mirror and said:

"This is me. And I'm okay."

No apologies. No caveats. No conditions.

Just… me.

And for the first time since this journey began, I wasn't waiting for someone else to validate it. I had done that for myself.

CHAPTER SIX

My Son Saved Me

If you've never had to explain cancer to a child, you won't know the impossible weight of trying to sound strong while your voice is cracking from the inside.

My son was five when the worst of it began. Kindergarten. Spelling words. Crayons on the floor. Sticky fingers and belly laughs and bedtime stories.

He was still asking me to tie his shoes. Still calling me "Mommy."

He didn't know what cancer was.

And I didn't want him to.

I didn't want to place that fear in his little heart. I didn't want to paint his childhood with hospital lights and the smell of antiseptic and the sound of beeping machines. I wanted to keep his world whole. Normal. Innocent.

But how do you hide a monster this big?

At first, we kept it simple. "Mommy's not feeling well." "Mommy's going to the doctor again." "Mommy has to rest."

And he accepted it. Because children believe what their parents tell them, especially when it's wrapped in a kiss and a smile.

When I came home after one of my longer hospital stays, I knew what was coming. The treatment had already begun to take its toll. My hair, once thick and strong, was thinning fast, falling out in strands on my pillow, in the shower, in my hands. I didn't want to watch it disappear slowly. I wanted to take control.

That morning, my husband dropped our son off at school and then came to the hospital to bring me home. We didn't speak much on the ride back. We didn't need to. The silence was its own kind of tenderness.

When we got home, I sat in the living room floor and handed him the clippers.

"I'm ready," I told him. "Let's do it before he gets home."

He nodded, but I could see the tears in his eyes before the first buzz began.

And when the first lock fell, he broke.

He tried to keep going, but his hands were shaking. He was sobbing, stopping every few seconds to catch his breath, wiping his face with his sleeve, trying to steady himself while I sat there, calm as ever, telling him, "It's just hair. It's okay. I'm okay."

I was the one losing it and still, I had to be the strong one.

We had to take breaks. Not for me, but for him.

Because watching someone you love go through this isn't passive. It shatters you in slow motion.

And that moment, my husband on the floor, clippers in hand, tears falling faster than the hair, was the most love I've ever felt.

Not because he cried.
But because he stayed.
Because he did it anyway.

Because he loved me enough to fall apart in front of me and still finish the job.

When our son returned that afternoon and saw me for the first time, his wide eyes and trembling voice nearly unraveled me. But somehow, through his innocence, through his unfiltered spirit, he found a way to make me laugh again.

And in that laughter, something inside me shifted.

In that moment, I realized: I still had purpose.
I still had light to protect.
I wasn't done.

He never saw my pain. Not fully. I hid it in the shower,

behind closed doors, in the hours after he fell asleep. I protected his innocence the way a lioness protects her cub; fiercely and without apology.

But children sense things. And one day, over FaceTime while I was still hospitalized, he looked at the screen and said, "Mommy,

I miss you so much. I just want to give you a big hug and a kiss."

That broke me.

I turned to my husband and said, "Bring him. I don't care how I look. I need him."

And so began the visits, two or three times a week. After school, he would ride into the city and crawl into my hospital bed like it was the couch at home. He'd read his books to me. I'd help with his homework. We'd watch cartoons on my hospital room TV.

For those brief windows of time, I wasn't a cancer patient. I was just Mommy again.

When I couldn't walk to the bathroom on my own, he held my hand and walked beside me. His little palm wrapped around my fingers with a gentleness beyond his years. He never asked why I was stitched together. He only ever asked if I was okay.

One day, he looked at the bandages across my chest and whispered, "Does it hurt?"

I lied.

I said, "Not anymore."

Because I needed him to feel safe, even when I didn't.

There were nights I wanted to give up. Nights when the pain screamed louder than my will. When the depression crept in like fog and I couldn't see a reason to keep going.

But every time I came close to surrender, I pictured him. I saw his face. His little hands. His drawings on the fridge.

I thought, If I leave, I take his sunshine with me. And that? That I could never do.

He saved me. Not with medicine or therapy or lectures. But with his presence. With the sound of his laughter. The smell of his skin. The way he still looked at me like I was a superhero, even when I felt like a patchwork quilt of pain and scars.

He never saw brokenness. He saw Mommy.

And because he did…Eventually, I did too.

One day, not long ago, he came home from school beaming with pride. "We had to draw a picture of our mommies," he said, holding up a piece of paper. He had drawn me, bald, strong, standing tall, in a cape.

"You're my superhero," he said. "Because you beat the monster."

I hung that drawing on the fridge.

Because that's when I knew...I hadn't just survived for myself. I had survived for him. And that made every single scar, every surgery, every tear, every step of the journey worth it.

JS

CHAPTER SEVEN
I Wanted to Die *(But Chose to Live)*

Most people who knew me back then would say I was strong. They saw me mothering through surgeries, smiling through pain, fighting with grace. But there were parts of my journey I didn't let anyone see. Not even my son. Not even my husband. Because behind the strength was a silence I didn't know how to voice, a darkness I didn't know how to name.

Let me be clear: I never feared death. But I did flirt with the idea of surrender. Not because I was weak. Not because I lacked fight. But because there are moments, moments that come in the silence, in the stillness, in the dark, when the weight of pain feels heavier than the worth of breath.

That moment came for me after one of my major surgeries. I had just been transferred back to my hospital room. The anesthesia was wearing off, the reality setting in. I reached for my chest, instinct, maybe, and what I felt was… nothing.

No ribs. No breast. No shape I recognized.

Only pain. And silence.

I asked the nurse for a mirror.

When I finally looked, I didn't cry. I didn't scream.

I sank. Sank so deeply into the bed, into myself, that I wasn't sure I'd ever resurface. The woman staring back at me looked like a stranger stitched together from trauma. Frankenstein's twin. Swollen, discolored, missing pieces. I couldn't reconcile the image with the version of myself I had known. I kept blinking, as if the mirror was lying. As if the woman I had been was still under there, somewhere, waiting to emerge.

But she wasn't. She was gone.

The thoughts didn't come all at once. They were quiet. Creeping.

"Maybe this is too much."

"Maybe they'd be better off without seeing me like this."

"Maybe surviving isn't worth it if this is what it looks like."

I never said them out loud. Not at first. But they echoed. Louder with each day I spent tethered to IVs, barely able to move, aching from inside the bones I no longer fully had. I wasn't afraid of dying. I just couldn't see the point of living like this.

That's the part people don't talk about enough, the gray

space between survival and surrender. The space where your body is still here, but your spirit… wavers.

The only person I told at first was Sophia. She's more than a best friend, she's family. The godmother of my son. The kind of woman who would drop everything in her life, including caring for her own mother with dementia, to drive five hours just to hold my hand in silence. And she did. Over and over again.

When I couldn't speak, she stayed on the phone while I sobbed. When I said, "I don't think I can do this anymore," she didn't panic. She listened. She didn't try to fix me. She reminded me I wasn't alone.

It was Sophia who gave me the courage to finally tell my husband what I was feeling. The courage to walk into the psychologist's office at MSK and say, "I need help."

And that was the first step.

I met with a therapist twice a week for nearly two months. At first, I hated it. I didn't want to talk. I didn't want to dig. But session by session, something began to shift. Not because she gave me any magical answers, but because she gave me space. Space to be angry. To be sad. To say, "I hate this." To ask, "Why does everyone keep telling me I'm strong when I don't feel strong?"

She let me grieve, not just the loss of my body, but the loss of identity, routine, independence. The loss of "normal."

And then one day, I walked into her office, sat down, and said:

"This is my last session."

Not because I had been fixed. But because I had made a choice.

I was done sitting in the story of my pain. I was ready to write the next chapter. I told her, "I'm not going to cry about this anymore. I'm not going to let these scars hold me hostage. I don't want medication. I want my mind back."

That was the moment I reclaimed my power.

I didn't need to be healed to begin again. I just needed to decide.

After that, things didn't magically become easy. But I began to move with a different energy. I saw my son with clearer eyes. I laughed more, real, belly laughs that cracked through the silence. I sang, even off-key. I started walking again. Lifting again. Living again.

And every time the voice in my head whispered, "You'll never be whole again", I whispered back:

"Watch me."

I didn't choose cancer. But I chose everything that came after.

I chose to stay.
I chose to live.

I chose to look at the ugliest version of myself in the mirror and say:

"You are still worthy of joy."

"You are still capable of love."

"You are still here, and that is enough."

CHAPTER EIGHT

The Decision: No More Surgeries

After the last surgery, I was left with a body that didn't just feel foreign, it felt finished. Not in a defeated sense. In a complete sense. There had been so many procedures by then, so many incisions, grafts, drains, staples, stitches. My body had become a roadmap of survival. A living collage of endurance. A memory etched in flesh.

But the world doesn't like unfinished stories, and to everyone else, I looked unfinished. Doctors, friends, even well-meaning strangers would ask:

"So... when's your reconstruction?"

"Are they going to fix it?"

"Are you getting your breast back?"

As if something was missing. As if I couldn't possibly be okay as I was. But here's the truth they didn't see: I wasn't waiting to be whole. I was whole.

Still, I entertained the conversation. Because I owed it to myself to be sure. That's how I found myself sitting in Dr.

Jonas Nelson's office again, the man who had skillfully performed the last of my major surgeries, who had stitched me back together when my body had nearly given out.

He walked into the room with his usual steadiness, carrying scans and options. He spoke clearly, carefully, respectfully.

"If you choose to go through with reconstruction," he said, "you'll likely need three or four more surgeries. Maybe more. And even then, the result won't be perfect. The skin we grafted from your thigh may not survive the next procedure. If it fails… we'd need to harvest from another site."

He paused.

And in that pause, I heard everything he wasn't saying.

You've been through enough.

There may not be anything left to give.

You don't have to keep going just to meet someone else's idea of "complete."

I remember the silence in that room like it was a character in the story. I looked at him. He looked at me. I could see in his eyes that he already knew what I was about to say.

"No more," I said, my voice clear and calm. "No more surgeries. This is it. This is who I am now."

And I meant it.

Not out of defeat. Not out of fear. Out of conviction.

That night, my husband and I sat on the couch, shoulder to shoulder, and talked about everything. I told him the details, the risks, the recovery time, the pain, the unknowns.

He listened.

And then he looked at me with that unwavering calm he always carried, the kind of quiet strength that holds you up when your own legs are tired.

"I love you like this," he said. "You don't need to go through more for me. Or for anyone."

That's when I knew I had made the right call.
But it was our son who sealed it.

He came into the room and threw himself into my lap, all limbs and joy, and said, "You're the strongest mommy in the world."

He didn't care that I only had one breast.
He didn't see what was missing.
He saw what remained.

Over the next few months, I made it my mission to not just recover, but rebuild. I trained harder than ever. Not to look good in a mirror, but to feel powerful in my own body. I wasn't training to be beautiful. I was training to be unstoppable.

They told me it would take eighteen months to regain my strength.

I did it in eight.

Eight months of sweat, discipline, grit. Eight months of pushing through scar tissue and muscle loss and mental exhaustion. Eight months of proving to myself that I wasn't just surviving anymore.

I was thriving.

And something else happened in that time: people began to notice. Doctors. Nurses. Fellow survivors. Trainers. Strangers. They saw the body that had once been labeled "too far gone" transform into something extraordinary. Not perfect — but powerful.

Dr. Nelson was stunned. Every time I came in for a checkup, he shook his head in disbelief. "You should be on a stage," he said once. "Telling this story. Showing what's possible."

Eventually, he asked if he could share my journey at medical seminars. He believed that what I had done, physically, mentally, spiritually, could inspire not just other patients, but the doctors treating them.

I said yes. Because this wasn't just about me anymore.

I started filming my workouts. Not for likes. For proof. Proof that a woman with one breast, missing ribs, and a map of scars could still lift. Could still dance. Could still live.

Women started reaching out. They wanted to know what I was doing. How I had healed. How I had chosen to stop chasing someone else's idea of normal.

And I told them the truth:

"I chose peace over perfection. I chose power over pain. I chose me."

Of course, I still have hard days. I still feel that phantom ache where my ribs used to be. I still catch my reflection sideways sometimes and have to remind myself: You're okay.

But more often than not? I walk past the mirror, flex my arm, smile, and keep moving.

Because I didn't just say no to more surgeries.

I said yes to this life.
This body.
This story.

Exactly as it is.

CHAPTER NINE
The Workout That Healed Me

Healing isn't always found in a hospital. Sometimes, it's found in sweat. In music playing too loud through earbuds. In the burn of your muscles shaking at the end of a set. In the quiet discipline of showing up for yourself over and over again.

After I made the decision to stop pursuing more surgeries, I felt a strange kind of freedom. For the first time in a long time, I wasn't preparing for the next hospital visit, or anticipating the next scar.

I had spent so long enduring. Now, I wanted to rebuild.

But not just physically.

I wanted to reconnect with the woman I had been before cancer, not the version defined by appearance, but the one defined by power. The woman who felt grounded in her strength. Focused. Unstoppable.

I started small. Ten-minute walks. Gentle stretching in bed. Breathing deep enough to fill my lungs without pain. Each movement felt like reclaiming territory. Not from cancer, but from fear.

Doctors told me to wait. "You'll need a year and a half to regain your strength," they said. "Ease in slowly. Start with therapy. Be careful."

And I nodded. **Then went to war.**

Because I wasn't interested in waiting to feel alive again. I wasn't reckless, but I was relentless. I listened to my body like it was gospel. I gave it what it could handle. Then just a little more.

Day by day, I got stronger.
Not prettier. Not slimmer.

Stronger.

That was the only metric that mattered to me.

I began training regularly again, lifting weights, rebuilding lost muscle, moving my body in ways that made me feel present in it again. At first, it was awkward. Some movements were impossible. Some days I cried in between sets. Some mornings I couldn't lift a grocery bag without a reminder of what had been taken.

But I kept going.

And slowly, my body caught up to my will.

I started filming my workouts, not for praise, but for proof. For myself. For other women. For anyone who needed to see that a body with scars is still a body with power.

Soon, people began to notice. Women at the gym approached me. Some were older, some survivors themselves, some just curious.

"Are you a trainer?"

"No. I'm a survivor."

Their eyes would light up. "Can I train with you?"

Always, my answer was yes.

Not for money. For meaning.

I began coaching women. Not professionally. Not with contracts or business cards. Just with heart. They'd come to me with all the usual hesitations:

"I can't do that. I'm too old."
"My body hurts."
"I'm not strong like you."

And I'd tell them, every single time:

"Don't tell your body what it can't do. Show it what it can."

We'd start simple. Breathwork. Light reps. Affirmations.

And I watched them transform, not just physically, but mentally. Because the real strength isn't in the squat. It's in the mindset that you deserve to try.

I trained through tenderness. Through tightness. Through the lingering aches where ribs used to be.

And every morning, I told myself:

"I can do it."
"I will do it."
"I am strong."
"I am happy."
"I am healing."

And guess what?
It worked.

Not perfectly. Not painlessly.
But it worked.

There are still days I wake up stiff. Days when the mirror reminds me of what I lost. Days when the phantom pain returns and whispers, "This is forever."

But I lift anyway.

Not because I'm chasing a version of myself from the past. But because I'm honoring the woman I am now. Because motion is medicine. Because every rep, every drop of sweat, every stretch of skin over scar, is a declaration:

I'm still here. And I'm stronger than ever.

JS

CHAPTER TEN
Teaching Others, Training the Mind

At first, I trained for survival. Then I trained for strength. But somewhere along the way, something shifted: I started training for others. Not just to inspire them, but to equip them. To remind them that strength isn't a luxury for the elite. It's not just for athletes or the lucky or the unscarred. Strength is a right. A calling. A mindset. And everyone has access to it, if they're willing to speak it into existence.

People started coming to me more often. At the gym. At the store. Online. Through friends. Through whispers.

"She's the woman who survived all that… and still trains like a beast."

They weren't just curious about what I was doing. They wanted to know how.

"How do you stay so motivated?"
"How do you push through the pain?"
"Weren't you scared to start again?"
"Do you still feel broken?"

And my answer, every time, was simple:

"It's the mind. Not the mirror."

You see, people think healing starts in the body. But that's backwards. It starts in the brain. Like my friend, Adrian, always says, **"The body cannot do what the mind doesn't already believe."**

You can do all the reps you want, eat the perfect diet, follow every protocol, but if you wake up every day and say, "I'm still broken," your body will believe you.

So I began teaching people how to train their thoughts before they ever picked up a weight. No more negative talk in the mirror. No more "I can't." No more apologizing for what your body looks like or what it's been through.

I taught them to say:

"I am strong."
"I am healing."
"My scars are proof, not shame."
"I can. I will."

Even if they didn't believe it yet, I made them repeat it until they started to feel it in their chest. Because the body doesn't move without permission from the mind.

The women I trained weren't bodybuilders. They were teachers. Moms. Nurses. Survivors. Women who had been told by life, or worse, by doctors — that their best physical days were behind them.

And every single one of them discovered something profound:

Their bodies weren't the problem. Their thoughts were.

Some of them were in their 50s and 60s. One of them had never stepped foot into a gym before we met. Another had just come through a divorce and hadn't felt like herself in years. Another was a breast cancer survivor who still couldn't look in the mirror without wincing.

Each one came with a story. With weight heavier than dumbbells. With a belief that maybe they were too far gone.

And one by one, I watched them lift, not just metal, but grief. Not just reps, but shame. I watched them rise.

One morning, a woman I had been working with for a few weeks came in and said, "You changed my life."

I shook my head.
"No," I told her. "You did. I just gave you permission."

And that's when I realized what I was really doing.

I wasn't training bodies. I was handing out keys. Unlocking belief.

I don't charge anyone for my time. If someone asks for help, I give it. Because I remember what it was like to be lost in a body I didn't recognize. To stare at myself and wonder if I'd ever feel powerful again. And I made a promise that if I ever climbed out of that place, I'd reach back and help someone else do the same.

So I do.

With every session. With every story I share. With every woman I remind: You're not too old. You're not too broken. You're just waiting for someone to remind you of who you are.

And still, people ask:
"How do you stay so positive?"

The truth? I don't. Not every day. There are mornings I wake up and feel the phantom ache in my chest. Nights I lay in bed and wonder what I would do if the cancer came back. Days when my scars feel louder than my smile.

But I train anyway.

Because I've learned that positivity isn't a mood. It's a muscle. And I've spent years building it.

I'm not perfect. But I am proof. Proof that healing is not linear. Proof that strength is not exclusive. Proof that training your body is really about training your spirit.

And if my journey can help someone else see their own strength then all of this? The pain. The loss. The war. It was worth it.

CHAPTER ELLEVEN

Financial Fallout & Moving to Florida

Cancer doesn't just attack your body. It attacks your bank account. Your plans. Your savings. Your idea of security. Your sense of control. And not all at once, slowly, like a tide that keeps rising while you're still trying to build sandcastles on the shore.

When people talk about surviving cancer, they talk about strength and chemo and surgeries and scans. They don't talk about what happens after. They don't talk about the letters in the mail. The insurance statements you don't understand. The credit cards you quietly max out. The job opportunities you have to say no to because your body can't handle one more thing. The pride you swallow when someone offers help, and you're too tired to say no.

When we sold our home in New York, it wasn't part of some master plan. It was a necessity. We needed the money. We needed a reset. We needed a chance to breathe in a place where the cost of living didn't threaten to choke us every month.

So we moved to Florida. Boca Raton. A new place. A new start. A new zip code with no memories of hospital rooms, no ghost of IVs in the hallway, no corner of the house that held the imprint of my pain.

We rented a modest apartment and enrolled our son in public school. I believed, truly believed, we'd bounce back quickly. I thought we'd find our rhythm, regain financial stability, and begin to rebuild.

But life had other plans.

My husband was starting over, too.

At 52, he was rebuilding a business from scratch in a brand-new city, knowing no one, carrying the weight of not just our future, but our past. He never complained. Not once. He poured everything he had into his work. Every ounce of himself. While I was healing, he was hustling. While I was recovering, he was holding the rest of our lives together.

But Florida wasn't easy. Clients were slow to come. Bills were not.

And soon, the money we'd made from the house was gone. Not from reckless spending, but from survival. Medical bills. Flights to New York for treatment. Follow-up scans. Groceries. School supplies. Rent. Life.

One day I looked at our balance and realized: We're at the edge.

We had no more cushion. No more backup plan.

And yet, he never showed it. He stayed steady. Faithful. Unshaken. I don't think I'll ever be able to fully express what that kind of love and endurance meant to me.

While I was physically broken, he never once let me feel financially abandoned. He carried us. But it cost him more than anyone knows.

Then came the hardest moment. After four years of ongoing scans, follow-ups, and care at Memorial Sloan Kettering, we simply couldn't afford the health insurance anymore.

Let that sink in.

I had survived cancer. But now, I couldn't afford to keep checking if it was still gone. I didn't even realize we had lost the coverage at first. It lapsed without warning, just another automatic payment that never processed because the account was stretched too thin. And by the time I found out, I had already missed appointments. I was, unknowingly, uninsured.

That reality sat on my chest heavier than any surgery. I didn't tell my husband at first. I didn't want him to feel like he had failed me. So I said something I had never imagined I would say:

"I think I'm fine. I don't need any more scans right now."

It wasn't true.
But it gave us breathing room.

That's the thing about the aftermath, it's filled with moments like that. Moments where you choose silence over honesty, not because you're hiding, but because you're protecting someone you love from a truth they can't fix. Moments where you put off your own needs to keep the roof over your head. Moments where strength looks like smiling through a storm.

I still lived with one breast. The plan had always been to eventually remove the other implant for symmetry. But now? That surgery wasn't just postponed, it was unreachable. We couldn't afford the luxury of closure. So I made peace with that too.

There were nights I cried quietly on the couch, where I had once slept during the worst of the pain. Not from fear. From frustration. From the emotional whiplash of surviving cancer… only to be buried by everything it left behind.

The world had moved on. I hadn't.

But something shifted about five months after one of those lowest moments. I stopped praying for escape. And I started praying for wisdom.

I stopped asking, "When will this be over?"

And started asking, "What am I supposed to learn from this?"

And when I made that shift, everything inside me calmed.

The external chaos didn't change overnight. We still had bills. Still had uncertainty. Still had long nights with no guarantees.

But inside? I found clarity. And in that clarity, I found strength again. Not the kind you post about. The quiet kind. The kind that helps you keep going when no one's clapping.

That's what this chapter of life taught me:

Sometimes healing doesn't look like hospitals or workouts or perfect endings. Sometimes it looks like staying put. Holding the line. Believing in the long game. Trusting that the storm will pass, even if it lingers longer than expected.

Eventually, the storm did pass.

And through it all, my husband never broke. He bore the weight of our future without complaint, pushed forward without applause, and never once stopped believing in the life we were fighting for. If today we are standing on steady ground, healthy, stable, and thriving, it's because he refused to quit. His resilience was our foundation and his unyielding work ethic paved the path for our current prosperity.

He is, and will always be, the rock of this family.

CHAPTER TWELVE
The Friends Who Carried Me

When people talk about survival, they talk about courage. They talk about grit. About strength. About pushing through when everything hurts.

But what they don't talk about enough, is community. About the people who show up quietly, consistently, lovingly, not to fix you, not to rescue you, but just to stand beside you while you figure it out.

I survived cancer.
But not alone.

And I never will say I did. Because there were moments I couldn't hold myself up. And in those moments, other people did it for me.

There was Tara, my neighbor back in New York. She lived across the street. Our sons were in the same first-grade class. We were friendly, not best friends. But when she heard what I was going through, something clicked in her.

Every single day, she picked up my son from school. Every single day, she fed him, watched him, kept him safe and smiling, while my husband and I were driving into the city for treatments, waiting in sterile rooms, sitting in traffic, praying for miracles. She never asked for anything in return.

Later, when I was hospitalized for months, in and out of surgery, wrapped in bandages and uncertainty, Tara made meatballs and sauce every single week and dropped them off at our door. So my husband and son would have something warm. Something familiar. Something that felt like love.

I cried when I heard. Not because I was sad. Because someone thought of me when I couldn't think for myself.

Then there was Flor and her husband Scott.

When we moved to Florida and I realized I'd still need to return to MSK in New York every few months for follow-up scans, I felt overwhelmed. We were scraping by. Travel expenses, hotels, Ubers, it all added up.

And then Flor said, "No. You'll stay with us."

Every time I flew up, she picked me up from the airport. She drove me to my appointments. She made sure I ate, slept, rested, and had zero extra stress. She did this every three months for four years.

Without ever asking for anything. Without once making me feel like a burden. That kind of love? That kind of humanity? You never forget it.

And then there was MJ. My angel in scrubs.

During my longest stretch in the hospital, she visited me
every day. Sat with me. Talked to me. Held my hand.

No agenda. No need for recognition.

She didn't flinch at my bandages. Didn't wince at the scars.
Didn't recoil from the IV poles or the smell of antiseptic.
She just showed up. Some days, she brought snacks. Other
days, we just sat in silence, watching the clock. Her presence
was a lighthouse when I was lost in the fog. She knew, even
if I didn't say it, that there's something holy about not being
left alone in your pain.

There was Sophia, of course. My sister-friend. My soul's
emergency contact. She drove five hours from Maryland,
over and over, just to sit on my couch and let me be
broken. She held me while I sobbed. Let me scream. Let me
say the darkest thoughts out loud without fear of judgment.

She never tried to "fix" me. She just held space. And that
space saved me.

And there was Dr. Bryan G. Forley.

He wasn't a neighbor or a friend in the traditional sense,
but he became something just as vital, a medical anchor in
the chaos. Most doctors perform a procedure and move on.
But not him. He stayed. Quietly. Gently. Consistently. He
checked in after I left his care. He called just to ask how I

was doing. He never treated me like a chart or a case file. He treated me like a person, one he refused to let fall through the cracks.

In the middle of my medical storm, he reminded me that even within the system, some people still see you. He never asked for credit. He never looked for thanks. But I carry his kindness with me. Because he didn't just catch what others missed, he held on when others might have let go.

I think about these people, and what they gave me, and I feel an ache in my chest that isn't from surgery. It's from gratitude. Because when I was too tired to carry myself, they became the scaffolding holding me together.

This is what people don't understand:

You can be strong. Fierce. Brave. But without people, the right ones, that strength has nowhere to land.

I had people. And their love didn't just comfort me. It transformed me. Because of them, I believe in paying it forward. Because of them, I offer help with no strings attached. Because of them, I cook for others when I know they're going through hell, because I know what it means when someone drops a meal at your door.

Because of them, I train women for free. I listen longer. I love louder. Because of them, I understand this truth deep in my bones:

Survival is not a solo sport.

So to Tara, Flor, MJ, Sophia, Dr. Forley, and the quiet army of others who prayed for me, held space for me, called me, fed me, fought for me... You didn't just help me survive. You reminded me why I wanted to survive. You reminded me I wasn't alone. You reminded me what love looks like when it shows up without being asked.

And I will carry your names with me... always.

CHAPTER THIRTEEN
Feeding Myself with Purpose

When your body has been to war, feeding it becomes an act of reverence. Food wasn't just food anymore. It was therapy. It was prayer. It was proof that I hadn't given up on myself.

After the surgeries, the medications, the long hospital stays and slow mornings, I knew that healing from the inside had to become my mission. The scars on the outside were obvious, but the inflammation, fatigue, and trauma inside needed just as much attention.

So I turned to nourishment like it was medicine. Because it was.

I began by asking a simple question:

"What would I feed someone I loved… who had just survived what I did?"

That's how I began treating myself. Not like a body to shrink. But like a soul to heal. I leaned hard into anti-inflammatory foods. Not because of a trend. But because my body was inflamed, tender, confused. I needed to calm the fire inside. I filled my plate with leafy greens. Berries.

Sweet potatoes. Omega-3 rich salmon. Avocados. Turmeric.

I replaced "low-fat" with full-healing. I swapped out sugar for honey. Coffee for green tea. Bread for grains that actually fed me, not just filled me.

And water?
Water became my lifeline.

I drank it like it was the only thing holding me together. Sometimes with lemon. Sometimes with mint. Sometimes plain. But always with purpose.

I gave up processed junk, not because I had to, but because my body had already survived so much that I refused to poison it with artificial things again. No more boxed "meals." No more drive-thru dinners. No more empty calories that looked like comfort but left me hollow.

I started cooking again. Slowly. Ritualistically. Even when it hurt to stand for long. Even when I had to prep with one arm gently hanging to my side, healing still.

Bone broth simmering on the stove.
Soup so gentle it felt like it was hugging my insides.
Small bites. Frequent meals. Gentle, steady healing.

Every meal became a message:

"I haven't given up on you."
"You're still worth feeding."

"You still have a life to live, and we're going to nourish you for it."

There were times when I didn't feel hungry, not physically.

But emotionally? I was starving for comfort. For routine. For care. For something in my day that wasn't pain or survival or managing bills or fatigue.

So I made food into ritual.
It became the thing I did for me, not just to me.

And when I say "feeding myself with purpose," I don't just mean the food. I mean the experience. The music playing while I cooked.

The deep breath I took before the first bite. The way I sat at the table, not scrolling, not rushing, but present.

Some days, I lit a candle. Others, I said a prayer.

I wasn't just eating.
I was honoring the miracle of still being here.

I also began teaching my son about this way of nourishment. Not just "eat your vegetables," but why. "Because your body is your one and only home," I told him. "Because what you feed it… becomes what it feeds you."

He didn't always understand. But I knew he would one day. And more than that, I wanted him to see me honoring my body. I wanted him to know his mother didn't punish her body with restriction. She restored it with intention.

To this day, my kitchen is where I heal the deepest. It's where I remember that I'm not broken. I'm rebuilding. And every plate I serve myself is another brick in the foundation of the woman I'm still becoming.

CHAPTER FOURTEEN

Finding Joy in a Scarred Body

For a long time, mirrors were my enemy. They reflected a reality I wasn't ready to embrace; a body stitched, hollowed, asymmetrical. A body that had once moved with fluid confidence, now learning how to exist in pieces.

I didn't cry every time I looked. Some days I didn't look at all.

Because looking meant acknowledging, and some days, I just didn't have the energy to be brave.

When you survive cancer, the world claps for your strength. But the applause fades when you're left standing alone in front of your reflection, naked, changed, and wondering...

"Am I still beautiful?"
"Am I still a woman?"
"Will anyone ever see me the same way again?"

But the real question, the one that matters more than all the others, is this:

"Will I ever see myself the same way again?"

And the truth? No. I won't.

Because the woman I was before cancer is gone. But the woman standing here now?

She's a fucking masterpiece.

I don't say that lightly. It took years, literal years, to say that sentence out loud. To look at the missing ribs, the scars across my chest and thighs, the skin that doesn't stretch the same, the places where something once was and now isn't… and smile.

But I can now.

Not because I look the same. Because I see differently.

I no longer look for flawlessness. I look for evidence.
That I fought.
That I lived.
That I stayed.

My scars are not damage. They are documentation.

A living, breathing testament to what I've endured. To what I've healed. To what I've chosen, over and over again, to rise from.

One day, I stood in front of the mirror, touched my chest, and whispered, "Thank you." Not because it was pretty. Because it was mine. Still alive. Still here. Still mine.

There is joy now in getting dressed. Not because I hide what I've lost, but because I no longer feel like I have to. I wear tank tops at the gym.I wear swimsuits at the beach. I wear sports bras when I train with other women, and I let them see the scar that runs across my chest like a lightning bolt. I let them see what survival looks like. Because if they see me, maybe they'll believe in themselves more too.

My son sees my body. And he never flinches. He hugs me and wraps his arms around my waist and says, "You're so strong, Mommy." He doesn't see what's missing.

He sees a warrior. And now, finally, so do I.

Some days, the tenderness returns. Some nights, I wake up and the ache in my chest reminds me there's no rib cage on one side. Just a soft sheet of skin between my heart and the world.

But I don't fear that anymore. I respect it.

Because it means I'm still here.And every beat of that exposed heart? It's a promise I made to myself:

To love this version of me.

Not eventually. Now.

I find joy in this body every single day. In the way I move. In the way I carry groceries by myself again. In the way I walk taller in public spaces without adjusting my clothes.

In the way I sing while I cook. Dance while I clean. Laugh too loudly at jokes that aren't even funny. In the way I show other women that joy is possible even here.

Especially here.

Because once you've seen your body torn apart and rebuilt…
You stop waiting for permission to feel beautiful.

You just decide that you are.

CHAPTER FIFTEEN
The Mirror, Revisited

After surviving cancer, I thought the hardest part was over. The scans, the surgeries, the drain tubes, the nights I prayed I'd wake up tomorrow... I had made it through all of that. I was alive. But no one talks about what happens after you survive. No one prepares you for the quiet moments when you're alone with your reflection, when the outside no longer matches the woman you used to know.

My hair had begun to grow back; awkward, patchy, and short. I'd stare into the mirror and see someone unrecognizable. Not a warrior. Not a survivor. Just... a stranger. A cute boy, maybe, I used to joke, but not the woman I had once been. And certainly not the one I wanted to see again.

We were still rebuilding financially. Every dollar was spoken for; groceries, rent, leftover medical bills. So spending money on something as "vain" as hair care felt impossible. Self-care felt like a luxury I couldn't afford, and the woman in the mirror paid that price every day.

Then came a phone call.

It was Maria, my longtime hair colorist and friend of more than two decades. Her voice, familiar and warm, cut through the shame I didn't realize I was carrying.

"Come in," she said. "Let me treat you."

I hesitated. I didn't want to feel like a burden. But she was insistent, in the best way.

When I walked into the salon, a giant bouquet of flowers was waiting for me. I almost cried right then and there. Maria greeted me with a hug that felt like home and guided me to her chair. There was no pity in her touch. No awkward small talk to fill the silence. Just kindness, quiet, unwavering, and real.

She colored my hair gently, thoughtfully, as if every strand was a prayer. And before I could even glance in the mirror, Sean, my longtime cutting stylist, stepped in. With precision and care, he began shaping the new growth, not just into a hairstyle, but into a possibility. When they were done, I didn't just look like me. I felt like me.

That day changed something in me. It wasn't about vanity. It was about identity. About wholeness. About seeing a version of myself I recognized; not the same, but familiar. Not perfect, but powerful.

Maria, you reminded me that beauty is not selfish. That it can be healing. That it can be holy.

Sean, you helped me finish the reflection I was afraid to face.

Together, you didn't just do my hair. You restored my spirit.

And in that moment, with the scent of shampoo in the air and my heart beating steady in my chest, I felt something I hadn't felt in a long time: beautiful.

And more than that... **worthy**.

CHAPTER SIXTEEN
This Is Why I'm Writing

At first, I started writing this story for me. Because the memories were tangled. Because the healing wasn't linear. Because the weight of it all had no place to go, except out of my chest and onto the page.

I didn't plan on making it a book.
I didn't think my story was "big" enough.

I wasn't famous. I didn't have a medical miracle. I wasn't the face of a foundation.

I was just... me.

A woman who had been through something horrific. A woman who chose to live. A woman with scars and strength and a whole lot of mess in between.

I doubted myself constantly. Who would want to read this? Who am I to write a book? What if people think I'm just seeking attention?

And then, one afternoon at a birthday party, I had a conversation that changed everything.

My friend Adrian, someone who had known bits and pieces of my journey, asked me, "Why haven't you written it all down yet?" I gave my usual excuses. And he said something I'll never forget:

"Jade, you keep saying that if your story helps just one person, it's worth it," he said. "But that's not good enough."

"Your story carries too much power, too much depth, to be measured in ones. Your story isn't meant to quietly inspire in passing, it's a story meant to move many... to shake people. To remind them what's possible. *Don't fucking minimize it.*"

That truth settled in my chest and rewrote the way I saw this whole process.

That night, I sat on the edge of my bed, opened my laptop, and stared at the blank screen. I didn't try to be poetic. I didn't plan chapters. I didn't outline or organize.

I just started telling the truth.

Messy. Honest. Raw.

The thoughts I hadn't spoken out loud. The questions I had asked myself at 3 a.m. The parts I was embarrassed to admit, not because of shame, but because they were real.

And the more I wrote, the lighter I felt. Not because the pain disappeared, but because it had somewhere to go. And then something even more powerful happened:

As I kept writing, I stopped thinking of this as my story.

I started thinking of her.

The woman sitting in a hospital gown, alone, terrified, trying not to cry in front of the doctor. The one who feels like a stranger in her own body. The one staring at her chest, wondering if her partner will still find her attractive. The one who feels like she has to "stay strong" for her kids, even when she's falling apart.

The one who feels guilty for surviving. The one who hasn't told anyone that she sometimes wishes it had just ended already, because at least then, the pain would be over. The one who looks fine on the outside but is silently battling the storm inside.

Her.

You.

Us.

This book is for her.

Because she deserves to know:
You are not broken.
You are not a burden.
You don't have to be fearless to be brave.

You don't have to look like you used to in order to feel beautiful.

You don't have to explain your pain.
You don't have to earn your healing.
You don't have to be perfect to be powerful.

I'm writing this because I remember what it felt like to feel invisible. To smile in public and cry in the shower. To post inspirational quotes while secretly wondering if I was falling apart.

I want this book to be the friend I didn't always have. The hand I wish had reached out in my lowest moment and said, "You are still here. Keep pushing. Keep fighting."

I'm not a therapist and definitely not a motivational speaker. I'm no guru, not a doctor, and I'm not an expert in healing.

But I am a woman who has walked through hell, and kept walking through the fire. A fire that broke me, and rebuilt me.

And if my journey can help you, or encourage you to keep walking through *your* fire, and get you out of your darkness, then every scar was worth it.

This is why I'm writing.

Not because my story is extraordinary. But because it's real.

And sometimes...

Real, is exactly what someone needs to feel seen.

A NOTE TO YOU

You Are Not Broken

If you are holding this book, still unsure about yourself…

Still unsure if you'll ever feel beautiful again.
Still unsure if healing is even possible.
Still unsure if anyone could ever understand what you're
going through…

Let me be the one to tell you:

You are not broken.

Not because you haven't been shattered. But because you
put yourself back together. Maybe not perfectly. Maybe not
completely. But intentionally. And that alone makes you
whole.

This story isn't just about cancer. It's about loss. About
identity. About rediscovering strength in places you thought
were permanently hollowed out. It's about choosing to wake
up and fight for joy, even when you don't feel ready. Even
when your reflection tells a different story. Even when your
body doesn't look like the one you used to love.

I've had days when I wanted to give up. Nights when I

stared into the dark and wondered what was left of me.

But each time I asked, "Am I still enough?" the answer came back, softly but clearly:

Yes.

So if you're still healing…
If you're in the middle of it, or just beginning, or years past your own battle and still learning to breathe again…

Please remember this:

You are not too late.
You are not alone.
You are here.

And that is enough.

ACKNOWLEDGMENTS

"Because Survival Is Never a Solo Story"

There is no such thing as surviving alone. Yes, I carried a heavy burden and fought harder than I thought possible. But I was never alone in this.

This book, and the life that made it possible, exists because of the people who refused to let me fall.

First and always, to Lewis, my husband – your strength never wavered, even when mine did. You held our lives together with quiet resilience and unconditional love. Through every treatment, every hospital stay, every setback, and every scar, you stayed. Thank you for loving me through it all, and for never letting me forget that I am whole, just as I am.

To my son Aidan, my reason – your innocence, laughter, hugs, and belief in me carried me through the darkest nights. I fought for you, I healed for you, and I live with purpose because of you. You are my miracle, and you'll always be the greatest thing I've ever had the privilege to hold.

To **Dr. Bryan G. Forley** – your care changed the course of my life. You didn't just perform a procedure. You listened.

You followed up. You stayed. In a medical world that moves fast and lets go too soon, you held space for me as a human being. I am here today because of your attention, your instinct, and your compassion.

Dr. Paul Tartter, Dr. Sharlotte Ariyan, Dr. Jonas Nelson, and every team member at Memorial Sloan Kettering who treated me with care, courage, and respect; thank you for taking on a case that was complicated, messy, and rare, and meeting it with heart. You fought for me medically so I could keep fighting emotionally. Thank you for being warriors in your own right.

To **Tara, Flor and Scott, MJ, Sophia**, and the army of friends who showed up, brought meals, picked up my son, made me laugh, held my hand, and never let me sit in silence, I will never forget you. You showed me what love looks like when it expects nothing in return. You carried me when I had nothing left. You were my light.

Maria, you reminded me that beauty is not selfish. That it can be healing. That it can be holy. **Sean**, you helped me finish the reflection I was afraid to face. Together, you didn't just do my hair. You restored my spirit.

To **Adrian**, my friend and editor, thank you for being the one person who told me the truth when I needed to hear it. You didn't let me shrink my story down. You challenged me to tell it fully, to honor it with every word, and to trust that what I had to say mattered. This book would not exist without you, and neither would my courage to finish it.

And finally, to every woman who reads this and sees herself in these pages, this book was written for you.

You are more than the pain, the scars, the doubt. And you are worthy of healing, of joy, of strength, and of a future that still belongs to you.

From the bottom of my heart,

Thank you.

Jade

MY BODY, MY PROOF
What I Chose to Show You

The following images are not here for shock value.

They are here because this is what survival actually looks like.

The scars, the pieces removed, the hair that once fell, they are not signs of weakness. They are proof of what was endured.

I chose to include these photographs not because I need your sympathy, but because I need you to see the truth.

These are not wounds. They are evidence.

They are mine.

And I am still here.

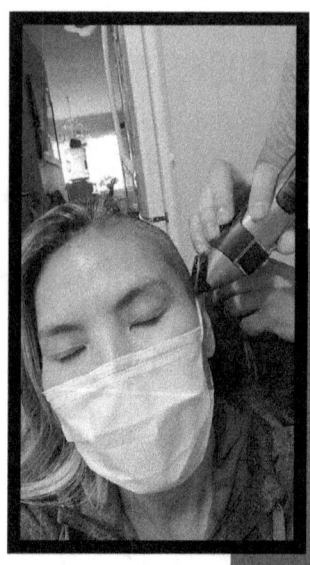

MY BODY, MY PROOF

The day I took back control.
Lewis held the clippers while
I held my strength. I lost my
hair, but not my fight.

That pile on the floor?
That wasn't loss.
That was liberation.

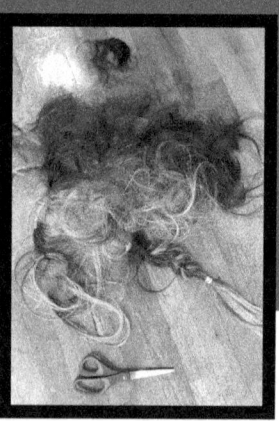

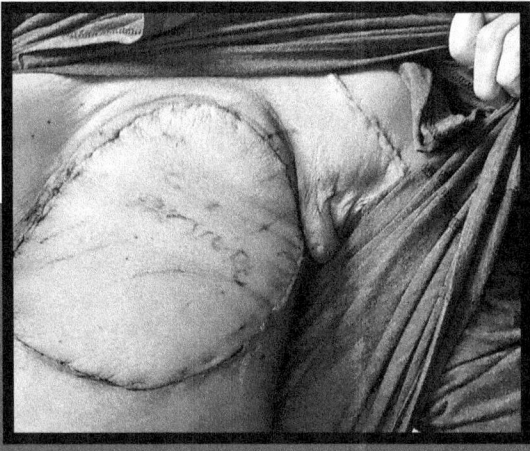

The part of my chest where ribs and muscle were removed.
There is no armor left between my heart and the world.
Just a thin veil of grafted skin and relentless courage.

This is my left thigh where
they harvested skin and
muscle to rebuild what
cancer took.

I walk differently now. Not
because I'm weaker... but
because I carry proof of
survival in every step.

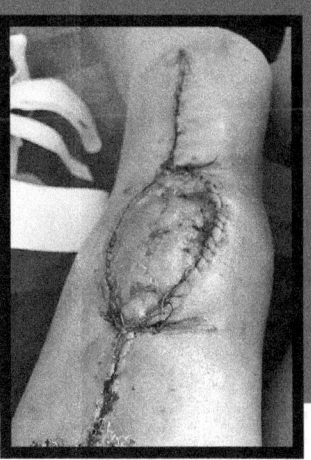

We are not the scars that we wear.
We are the strength that rises beneath them.

Adrian Pinzon Gallo